C000109298

Reading Fortune Telling Cards

This English edition copyright © 2021 U.S. Games Systems, Inc.

All rights reserved. The illustrations, cover design, and contents are protected by copyright. No part of this book may be reproduced in any form without permission in writing from the publisher, except by a reviewer who wishes to quote brief passages in connection with a review written for inclusion in a magazine, newspaper or website.

Originally published in 2018 by Para-Astra in the Dutch language

English Translation by Ruth Gistelinck

First Edition

10   9   8   7   6   5   4   3   2

Made in China

Published by
U.S. GAMES SYSTEMS, INC.
179 Ludlow Street
Stamford, CT 06902 USA
www.usgamesinc.com

FABIO VINAGO

Reading Fortune Telling Cards

A Romani Approach Featuring the Gypsy Witch® Deck

Contents

1
The Romani Culture

Romani people are greatly admired for their impressive reputation as fortune tellers. They perfected the art of predicting the future with playing cards and evolved it into a full-fledged profession. The Romani people occupy a special place in divination history. They refined classical fortune telling with ordinary playing cards into a true art form. They gradually added all kinds of images to these playing cards, which have come to be associated with the Romani culture.

"Zigeuner" cards or Gypsy* cards, all belong to the same family, but the Gypsy cards have a very old history and are in no way comparable to any other divination methods.

The origin of this tradition is not yet fully known. There has been a lot of speculation throughout the years, but I personally have a strong opinion about the history of Gypsy cards. Over time, many fortune telling cards have been given the name "Gypsy" or "Gypsy Cards." The typical Gypsy cards are the only cards that are depicted with the inserts of the 52 regular playing cards in combination with 52 different images.

This combination of 52 cards and 52 card images cannot be found in any other divination system. The Romani have given it their own and unique meaning. They are proud people who want to distinguish themselves and this also applies to their divination techniques, which differ considerably

*Since this book discusses a specific type of deck and method of reading with Gypsy cards, (and is illustrated with the Gypsy Witch Fortune Telling Playing Card Deck) the term Gypsy cards is used here with the awareness and understanding that the term holds cultural connotations, which some readers may be sensitive to.

from the Lenormand method, for example.

The only resemblance that their technique bears to the classical Lenormand method is the essence, namely the combination of suits and card images and the placement of the cards: are they positioned to the left or right, above or below, far away or close in relation to the person card?

But certain card images, suits or positions have a positive meaning in one method and a negative meaning in the other or vice versa. In my work as a card reader, I have learned over the years that there are no right or wrong answers. Of course, the basic meanings within a method are always maintained, but the additional meanings that you wish to add will entirely depend on personal view points and intuition. You should see card reading as something that widens your horizon as well as the querent's.

A card like "the Fox" will always be a fox. You will not immediately associate it with something positive, unless you experience cunningness as positive. It remains a negative card with a touch of unreliability. In other card systems, the playing card linked to the fox is the nine of clubs whereas the Gypsy cards use the ace of hearts. Why this difference?

This is the typical Romani way of fortune telling. As mentioned above, they want to differentiate themselves and leave their mark. In my experience, their way of reading the cards gives very accurate and detailed interpretations. It extends your scope as a card reader because it reaches further and deeper. As a matter of fact, it adds an extra dimension to the knowledge that you derive from other fortune-telling techniques.

If we take a moment to look at the regular playing cards that the trueborn Romani used to make amazing predictions, we can see that every card had both a positive and negative meaning. According to their method, a negative or positive card impacts the surrounding cards in such a way that it reinforces or weakens the meaning of other cards.

My fascination with fortune telling has motivated me to write the book that you are now holding in your hands. *Reading Fortune Telling Cards* gives you insight into the Romani fortune-telling method and will teach you how to work with the Gypsy cards. I hope to inspire you all in the same way as I found my inspiration, which led to the development of a successful card-reading business.

Fabio Vinago

2
Card Layout

Each card is subdivided into:

1. Playing card suit: hearts, spades, diamonds or clubs

   Hearts are predominantly positive and say something more about the emotions of others and ourselves. What makes us feel good and what doesn't? Friendships and relationships are also interpreted according to these heart cards.

   Spades are neutral cards that show blockages such as uncertainties, stubbornly clinging onto something, control issues and fear of failure. In short, everything we project from our karma to the outside world. They also show us misunderstandings and lack of clarity.

   Diamonds are predominantly positive. They refer to our achievements, wealth and everything related to status and fame. Important decisions that we must take are also shown. According to the Romani method, the diamonds mainly speak of money and finances.

   Clubs are predominantly negative. They show us disturbed communication, discord and jealousy, worry, fear, panic, divorce and anger. Or the envy we feel towards others. According to the Romani method the clubs are also called "battle cards."

2. Card meanings: Number of keywords are linked to each card image to describe their meaning. For example: "The Sun" is associated with happiness, success, popularity and joy. "The Key" relates to finding solutions, gathering insights, and so on.

3. Placement of the card in relation to the other cards: this determines which other cards are reinforced or weakened. It is therefore essential to include the surrounding cards in the interpretation as they provide more details about a specific situation. Are they distant or near? Underneath or above the person card?

3
Working with the Gypsy Cards

Basic Rules

- Never lend your cards to anybody.
- Work in a dedicated card reading space.
- Burn a candle and/or an incense stick.
- Shuffle the cards before use or have them shuffled.
- Fan out the cards.
- Have the querent draw the cards following the method that you use.
- Spread the cards according to the methods explained in this book.
- Do NOT fan out the cards when doing a Grand Tableau.

Position of the cards and their influence on the timescale:

- To the left of the person card = past
- Above and under the person card = present, karma or destiny
- To the right of the person card = future
- Diagonals = what needs to be done
- Connector cards = a card that touches another card directly to the left, right, top, bottom or at one of the card corners.

Reading the Gypsy Cards

In addition to interpreting the card images, we also check which suits have the upper hand in a spread. If predominantly hearts, it tells us something about feelings, emotions, friendships, etc.

If there are mainly diamonds and clubs, the card images will show us whether there are concerns about money matters, problems at work or with a business, and so on.

We always read combinations of images and suits as this will give us a detailed story. Intuition is key here. I recommend that you get a good understanding of the card images and their keywords first before you include the suits. Suits require a different approach and might confuse you in the beginning.

Start small and finish big, that is my motto. By that I mean: practice the easy spreads before moving on to a Grand Tableau. Write down all the impressions that you get and keep a notebook if necessary.

Finally, I would like to add the following: Never compare the Gypsy cards with another deck such as Lenormand. Gypsy cards have their own specific, unique meanings. Comparing them will only cause confusion as several cards have different meanings in both systems.

Simply put, this means that Gypsy cards need to be read and interpreted according to a different method.

Let's have a look at card 40, Queen of Clubs, "The Wine."

This is a positive card. It refers to the joy of the small things in life, but also the cheerfulness that you can experience in a certain situation. It is therefore not as negative as the meaning that is usually associated with the Queen of Clubs in other fortune-telling systems. This card is also a person card and if we look at the playing card insert in this context, it symbolizes a lonely and bitter woman. In that case the clubs prevail again.

At the end of this book you will find a complete guide to all kinds of card combinations.

The layout of the Gypsy Cards

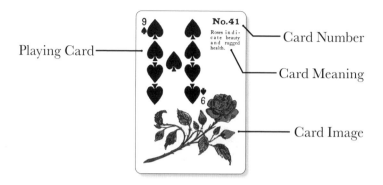

Playing Card

Card Number

Card Meaning

Card Image

The Gypsy cards are always read in two consecutive and different ways, based on the card images. The **first reading teaches** us what is currently happening with regards to the person. As an example, on the card above, we see the card image "The Roses." This is a symbol that refers to appearance and beauty, or to someone who always wants to look good. Keep in mind to always be discreet when talking about people's appearance.

The **second reading focuses** on the playing card insert, in this case, the Nine of Spades. Spades refer to uncertainties, blockages and the clinging to something or someone. They point to fear of failure and the constant search for validation. Reading "The Roses" and the Nine of spades together, we are looking at someone who always wants to look good, (they are insecure), wants to feel beautiful in the outside world (fear of failure) and who stubbornly clings to their own ideals (fear of losing control).

The meanings of the 52 Gypsy Cards

Card 1 • The Sun
Playing Card • Three of hearts
Keywords • Happiness, success, popularity and joy

"The Sun" always brings happiness. Near the person card, this indicates happiness and prosperity in all undertakings. The surrounding cards will explain where this joy is coming from. Are there love cards close by? Are there mainly cards of the suit of hearts? In that case, happiness is on its way in the love or friendship department. If "The Sun" has been dealt in one of the corners touching the person card, fated happiness is coming to the querent. Close to "The Snake," "The Mice" or the dark side of "The Clouds," there will be disappointment.

Card 2 • The Moon
Playing Card • Five of hearts
Keywords • Happiness, emotions, work

When close to the person card, "The Moon" is a card that promises a successful outcome of work, relationship or finance related matters. When "The Moon" is far from the person card and surrounded by negative cards, it predicts overwhelming worries. In proximity of "The Sun," these concerns will be alleviated. "The Moon" typically refers to our emotions. The surrounding cards will give more information.

Card 3 • The House
Playing Card • Six of hearts
Keywords • Success, prosperity, a stable marriage, our home

"The House" refers to our homelife in the broadest sense of the word, including our love life and friendships. "The House" is a pleasant and fruitful card that predicts a positive outcome. If you are currently in an unpleasant situation, your future will be happier and more prosperous, and everything will fall into place. "The House" is also the wedding card if card 42, "The Heart," touches one of the card corners.

Card 4 • The Key
Playing Card • Four of clubs
Keywords • Solutions and gaining insights, which door do you want to open?

"The Key" as a card shows solutions. The Gypsy proverb says: "A golden key fits on every door." How are you going to use 'The Key?' And which door do you want to open? With this card, we also need to check the cards immediately around it. This is how we gain insight into what is needed to fulfill a specific wish. The closer this card falls to the person card, the easier and faster the solution will be. When distant, there is still a long way to go. Don't lose heart!

Card 5 • The Tree
Playing Card • Three of clubs
Keywords • Good health, strength and success

Unlike the Tree in Lenormand, this card carries a positive meaning. "The Tree" stands for strength. It points to the fulfillment of our inner wishes. This is definitely the case when "The Flowers" are near; then our heart's wish becomes reality. Whether your wish involves love or work, fulfillment is heading your way. "The Tree" also indicates optimal health when surrounded by other positive cards.

Card 6 • The Coffin
Playing Card • Five of spades
Keywords • Loss, illness, acute and unfavorable circumstances

"The Coffin" shows us a sudden loss, which can occur in any area of life: money, relationships, health. The nature of the loss is indicated by the surrounding cards. When "The Coffin" is placed at the top, left, bottom or in one of the card corners, it points to the sudden end of a certain situation. Far away from the person's card, the end can be prevented if we consider "The Key" to determine what is required to positively influence the future and avoid misfortune.

Card 7 • The Flowers
Playing Card • Ten of hearts
Keywords • Long-term happiness, feeling good, sincere feelings and emotions

"The Flowers" is a card that predicts a long and happy life. You are also appreciated for what you do. People look up to you. This card has a positive effect after a series of negative cards. "The Flowers" also show us our own attitude to life, such as our concern for others. But watch out for excesses.

Card 8 • The Scythe
Playing Card • Ten of diamonds
Keywords • Disappointments, break-ups, the end

"The Scythe" is a card that predicts disappointments, break-ups and disillusionments. It shows an end to a certain situation. Unfortunately, you can never ignore this card. It always predicts sadness and loss. If there are love cards close, the relationship is broken off. Check the exact location of "The Scythe" to find out who will cause the break-up. Is it close to the man or the woman? If there is a lucky card near "The Scythe," the luck will be cut off, or it will be short-lived.

Card 9 • The Birds
Playing Card • Ace of diamonds
Keywords • Misfortune, enemies, unreliable people

With "The Birds" we end up in an unfortunate situation, especially when positioned at the top, to the right or in one of the corners of the person card. You have to watch out for certain people around you. You might be better off avoiding them. If "The Birds" card is farther away and is surrounded by at least three positive cards, you will be made aware of it just in time and will still be able to positively influence the situation. If there are several negative cards around it, you will first experience misfortune and then become wiser afterwards.

Card 10 • The Pig
Playing Card • Three of spades
Keywords • Luck, abundance, ambitions

"The Pig" is a sacred animal according to the Gypsies. This card predicts happiness that consists of great abundance, but also the ambition to achieve something in life. Whatever situation you are currently in, this card always predicts a magnificent outcome. Whether near or far from the person card, "The Pig" will always give you what you want.

Card 11 • The Fox
Playing Card • Ace of hearts
Keywords • Cunning, falseness, hypocrisy, unreliability

"The Fox" represents an absolutely unreliable person that you must avoid. It points to mistrust and cunningness of people from your immediate environment or circle of acquaintances. Pay attention to whom you entrust with information or resources. Don't let the fox guard the henhouse. The closer this card falls to the person card, the greater the threat. If "The Fox" is far from the person card, its negative effect is limited. Yet, you still have to stay on your guard.

Card 12 • The Children
Playing Card • Queen of diamonds
Keywords • Kindness, naivety, friendship

"The Children" always bring joy and are a harbinger of friendly contacts. This card also stands for naivety and wants to warn you not to be too accommodating. Try to act with maturity. Do not blindly follow someone else's story. Whether this card is placed above, below, to the left, to the right or in one of the corners of the person card, it always reflects the good intentions of the people around you.

Card 13 • The Snake
Playing Card • Eight of clubs
Keywords • Enemies, disasters, failures, jealousy

"The Snake" remains a snake. In this deck "The Snake" also represents a toxic person who doesn't fail to make other people's lives miserable. It is someone you should avoid. "The Snake" is like a negative energy that can be very draining. The closer to the person card, the more careful you should be. Farther away from the person card, it warns not to let certain people into your life. Forewarned is forearmed because the snake is always ready to strike. Check out the surrounding cards; with love cards near, the querent needs to be on their guard for another person who could sabotage the current relationship out of jealousy.

Card 14 • The Rider
Playing Card • Jack of diamonds
Keywords • Good news, message of love, contact

"The Rider" is a messenger who brings us news. If this card is positively surrounded and positive cards predominate, we can expect to receive good news that will make us joyful and happy. With a majority of negative cards, there will most likely be conflict and discussion. When "The Rider" has been dealt to the left of the person card, it doesn't make sense to wait for news because the person you are expecting it from is stubborn. Placed above, below or to the right of the person card, the querent will be approached and won't need to take the first step. A negative card such as "The Scythe" near "The Rider" indicates that you may be cut off from news.

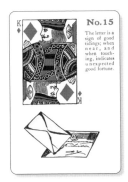

Card 15 • The Letter
Playing Card • King of diamonds
Keywords • Good tidings, surprise, spontaneity, a letter, text or email

"The Letter" brings us news in a spontaneous and surprising way. A message comes to you by means of a telephone call, a text, or another, indirect way of communication. This message is of great importance and has been expected for quite some time. If

"The Letter" is accompanied by "The Clouds," it is a negative message that can cause quite a bit of concern.

Card 16 • The Ship
Playing Card • Nine of hearts
Keywords • Wealth, financial aspects, trade, travel

"The Ship" is the symbol of financial wealth through trade, business or an inheritance. Positive things are being harvested regarding financial or trade matters. This card can also symbolize a journey if card 46 "The Railroad" is nearby. When "The Ship" is found above, below, to the right or in one of the card corners of a person card, its meaning is always work, trade or money related.

Card 17 • The Fish
Playing Card • Four of hearts
Keywords • Finances, materialism, success

"The Fish" is the financial card par excellence. It symbolizes someone who has achieved wealth and who explicitly pursues material prosperity. If "The Fish" are far away from the person card and surrounded by negative cards, there is a financial loss and you have to pay attention to what you will spend money on. However, if surrounded by positive cards, there will be a financial improvement.

Card 18 • The Lady
Playing Card • Two of diamonds
Keywords • For a female querent we always start from this card

This is "The Lady," used when we are performing a reading for a lady. We start from this card to find out what is surrounding her. And for the partner card, we look at card number 19, "The Gentleman," to find out how he relates to her.

Card 19 • The Gentleman
Playing Card • Two of hearts
Keywords • For a male querent we always start from this card

This is "The Gentleman," used when we are performing a reading for a man. We start from this card to find out what is surrounding him. And for the partner card, we look at card number 18, "The Lady," to find out how she relates to him.

Card 20 • The Lily
Playing Card • Seven of clubs
Keywords • Happiness, affection, family, virtue

"The Lily" forecasts a happy and virtuous existence. When "The Lily" is accompanied by "The Clouds," family issues cause us sorrow. Lying above the person card, "The Lily" points to a pleasant existence as a result of a happy family life. When placed under the person card, we should improve the way we set boundaries, and express values and norms. The cards to the right or left of the person card are taken into consideration to determine where the happiness will be coming from.

Card 21 • The Stork
Playing Card • Seven of hearts
Keywords • Changes for your own good, a move

"The Stork" denotes change or a move. The closer this card falls to the person card, the faster this move or change will take place. "The Stork" indicates that this change is needed and will positively influence your well-being and happiness. The change is simply necessary to improve your future. It is a positive card, even though it is not always read as such, because people are usually wary of change. However, you will reap the benefits at the end of the road. Change doesn't necessarily have to be bad; it can lead us to a different and better way of life.

Card 22 • The Book
Playing Card • Jack of hearts
Keywords • Mysteries, insights, revelations, new chapter

"The Book" helps you unravel a mystery and leads you to better and more accurate insights. It is a card that reveals things that make you wiser in life. Moreover, with this card you can turn a page in your life story. Is this card close to the person card? Then the truth will come to light very soon. If it is far away from the person card, it will take some time. If it lies around the person card, above, to the right, below or in one of the card corners, then you will unravel the mystery yourself.

Card 23 • The Ring
Playing Card • Queen of hearts
Keywords • Connection, relationship, marriage

"The Ring" is the typical relationship or commitment card. When "The Ring" is on the right side of the person card, it indicates that the person has a strong and rich relationship. He or she feels good about the partner in question. If "The Ring" is to the left of the person card, the relationship is not what it should be. When "The Scythe" appears as well, the relationship is doomed to be broken. Disappointments arise. In addition, we also look at the cards that have been dealt around "The Ring," regardless if it lies to the left or right of the person card. If "The

Ring" is on the right, surrounded by negative cards, this naturally points to a negative trend for the future.

Card 24 • Hand In Hand
Playing Card • King of hearts
Keywords • Trust, safety, compromises, clear communication

"Hand in hand" reflects a sense of trust and security. Whether it concerns a business or personal relationship, you can rest assured that the person in question has good intentions. "Hand in hand" also speaks of communication. It's a very positive card when favorably placed. With money cards close, it points to financial happiness and trust. When "The Snake" or "The Coffin" are around, it's better not to work with this person.

Card 25 • The Clouds
Playing Card • Seven of spades
Keywords • Divorce, conflict, emotional complications

"The Clouds" always bring trouble and emotional complications. This card also shows conflicts with others. These conflicts keep dragging on and eventually end up in drama. If the dark side of "The Clouds" (left) touches the person card or one of the love cards, it symbolizes a removal and separation between two people. If the light side of "The Clouds" (right) touches the person card or one of the love cards, it predicts peace,

32

prosperity and calmness after a period of severe adversity.

Card 26 • The Park
Playing Card • Nine of clubs
Keywords • Renewal, social contacts

"The Park" is a card that suggests new contacts. When distant from the person card and surrounded by negative cards, you must watch out for false friends. Pay attention to whom you are getting involved with; not everyone has good intentions. Close to the person card and surrounded by love cards, it indicates that a new love is approaching.

Card 27 • The Dog
Playing Card • Four of diamonds
Keywords • Sincere friendships, faithfulness, loyalty

"The Dog" signifies a loyal friend. In a spread this card also represents the sincere friends that you have gathered around you. When it touches one of the love cards, it symbolizes a trustworthy partner. "The Dog" is a loyal personality. If "The Dog" is surrounded by negative cards such as "The Clouds" or "The Snake," you must watch out for unexpected hostility of people in your close circle.

The anchor denotes successful ventures in business and love; and surrounded by 11, 13, 29, 30, 31, 35, breach of trust; near the dog, fidelity of the one you love.

Card 28 • The Anchor
Playing Card • Five of diamonds
Keywords • Anchoring, loyalty, success, love

"The Anchor" has a lasting effect on the positive cards surrounding it. This card can indicate success in business, but also loyalty in a relationship from the person you love. "The Anchor" expresses steadfastness and shows that you are doing everything you can to consolidate what you value. Don't worry too much, because love won't go away that easily. This card tells you that you don't have to worry unnecessarily.

The mouse denotes loss by theft; nearby, it denotes recovery after great difficulty; but distant, the loss will be irretrievable.

Card 29 • The Mice
Playing Card • Six of spades
Keywords • Loss, theft, bad luck

"The Mice" gnaw and indicate loss or theft. The theft can be of a financial nature (with "The Fish") but can also take place on an emotional (with "The Flowers") or relationship level (with a love card). If "The Mice" are far from the person card, you will soon be faced with a setback. When near, this loss can be prevented, provided that something is done with the surrounding cards.

Card 30 • The Rod
Playing Card • Ten of spades
Keywords • Quarrels, struggles, disagreements, communication

"The Rod" predicts arguments and struggles brought about by lingering disagreements and discussions. This card has a dominant edge, which means that both parties don't know when to stop. It refers to "the pot calling the kettle black." There is a lack of understanding and yes, what's done is done. With love cards nearby, there will definitely be a communication problem in the relationship. In the case of money cards, the conflict will be about finances and good communication will be needed to find solutions. Money and love don't mix!

Card 31 • The Roads
Playing Card • Ace of clubs
Keywords • Choices, adventures, weighing options, decisions

With "The Roads" we arrive at a crossroads. You have to make a choice, which inevitably creates a stressful situation. If the sunny side of the card (left) faces the person card, a choice is necessary to escape an approaching disappointment. The fight can still be avoided. If the other side of the card (right) touches the person card, the damage has already been done and you have to bear the necessary consequences. Which side do you choose? And what do you do with the advice you are being given?

The mountains nearby indicate the presence of a mighty enemy.

Card 32 • The Mountain
Playing Card • Eight of spades
Keywords • Enmity, difficulties, defying problems, challenges

"The Mountain" indicates obstacles that must be overcome. This card points to the presence of a powerful person in your surroundings who you need to watch out for. You simply have to stand up to your problems, but be wary of who you want to burden with this. Together with "The Dog," this card shows a negative and insincere friendship. In connection with love cards, this card tells you that you need to work on the problems in your relationship. Located near "The Fish" it is recommended to better manage your financial situation. You cannot ignore this card, and the fundamental message is: do not try to escape from your problems, tackle them!

The clover leaf is a bearer of good tidings; but if near clouds, it denotes great chagrin; if, however, No. 2 does not lie near 29 or 28, the chagrin will be of short duration and happiness will follow.

Card 33 • The Clover
Playing Card • Five of clubs
Keywords • Good times, happy feeling, our own emotions, positive news

"The Clover" is a card that promises us beautiful and happy times. This card wants us to enjoy what life has to offer. With "The Clouds" close, we can get cross and must learn to keep our emotions under control. Don't let fear and worry steal your joy. When "The Clover" is accompanied by "The Rider," you can expect good news.

We also look at the cards around "The Clover:" are they positive or negative? That tells us a bit more about how we approach life.

Card 34 • The Star
Playing Card • Two of spades
Keywords • Happiness, wishes, success in achieving your goals

"The Star" is a lucky card. Whether it concerns a love relationship, your own business or another wish, happiness is guaranteed to come to you. The closer "The Star" falls to the person or theme card, the sooner the result will follow. When distant, your patience will be put to the test and it will be a long-term effort. When "The Star" is surrounded by "The Clouds" or "The Mountain," you will go through a great ordeal before you find success.

Card 35 • The Tower
Playing Card • Ten of clubs
Keywords • Blockage, boundaries, inner struggle

"The Tower" indicates that you are dealing with an important blockage and that you are building a wall around you, making it difficult to allow people into your life. When this card lies close to the partner card, or near any love or feeling related cards, we can state that the partner experiences difficulties in expressing their feelings, which causes them to isolate themselves.

Card 36 • The Cat
Playing Card • Eight of hearts
Keywords • Cockiness, stubbornness, pride, unexpected

"The Cat" represents a vain personality. Someone who likes to be placed on a pedestal, but mainly lingers in their own world. It's a stubborn character that can come across as arrogant. When this card is related to a series of negative cards such as "The Snake" or "The Coffin" it speaks of a conflict with this person and you must be careful. Remember, a cat can strike unexpectedly and viciously.

Card 37 • The Rapiers
Playing Card • Ace of spades
Keywords • Watch out, be on your guard, threats, insults

"The Rapiers" indicate that you must watch out. Sooner or later you will be confronted with threats or insults. If this card falls close to the person card, it will be sooner rather than later. Farther away, it won't happen in the near future. This card has a very negative connotation, even after a series of positive cards. To be on your guard is the message!

Card 38 • The Flames
Playing Card • Seven of diamonds
Keywords • Neutralizing, luck, reinforces the positive cards

"The Flames" is the lucky card par excellence. This card is always positive and even neutralizes all surrounding negative cards. When this card falls close to positive cards, their meaning will be enhanced. Close to negative cards, the negativity emanating from them will be considerably weakened. This card is seen as the reinforcement of everything that makes us happy in life.

Card 39 • The Heart
Playing Card • Nine of diamonds
Keywords • Love, feelings, pleasure, joy

"The Heart" is the love card that predicts joy and happiness in everything that makes us feel good. Great luck is reserved for you, provided that this card is favorably placed. However, when we notice "The Mice" or "The Scythe," a break-up is guaranteed. With beautiful and positive cards around it, the relationship is good and genuine.

Card 40 • The Wine
Playing Card • Queen of clubs
Keywords • Cheerfulness, enjoying the little things, party

This card is downright positive. It makes us light-hearted and brings cheerfulness to our lives. "The Wine" also lets us enjoy the little things in life. This card knows how to have a party, especially when "The Park" is also present. Don't forget to consider the surrounding cards. When "The Wine" is accompanied by "The Heart," we get enjoyment from our relationship. With "The Park," we enjoy the social contacts that we maintain.

Card 41 • The Roses
Playing Card • Nine of spades
Keywords • Beauty, appearance, health

"The Roses" speak of our outer beauty. This card represents someone who always wants to look their best, and wants to be considered beautiful by the outside world. This may point to a certain degree of insecurity. Make sure that the concern over appearance doesn't become obsessive, as it is precisely because of this thinking that all kinds of uncertainties and doubts arise. When "The Heart" is present, we are talking about a great relationship. "The Roses" accompanied by "The Park" indicates that the querent wants to look their best and is seeking validation from others. This card is positive at its core but can also indicate vanity in certain cases.

Card 42 • Amor
Playing Card • Queen of spades
Keywords • Love, relationships, our own relationships

This is a very positive card. It highlights our own love relationship. Our partner craves and longs for us. The more positive the cards surrounding "Amor," the less need for worry.

However, when "The Snake" has been dealt to the right or appears in the left- or right-hand corner of "Amor," you need to watch out for evil tongues in the relationship. With "The Scythe," a break-up will be inevitable.

Card 43 • Lightning
Playing Cards • Six of clubs
Keywords • Unpleasant surprises, sudden events

"Lightning" represents an unpleasant event and things we do not expect. Bad luck hits us like a bolt in a clear sky. Vigilance is therefore required. When this card falls close to the person card, or touches the left- or right-hand corner, it will happen soon. We then have a look at the surrounding cards. Do we see mostly love cards, in combination with "The Scythe?" In that case, a total relationship breakdown will occur, which you hadn't anticipated.

Card 44 • The Broken Glass
Playing Card • Eight of diamonds
Keywords • Accident, the end, irreversible loss

"The Broken Glass" shows us a final end: something that is irreversibly lost. The situation we are in is not good for us and we must put an end to that. Are there any love cards? If so, the break-up will be permanent. When there are money cards around it, a financial loss will take its toll. The farther away from the person card, the less important the misfortune will be.

Card 45 • The Order
Playing Card • Jack of clubs
Keywords • Recognition, honor, labor

"The Order" stands for honor and appreciation, as well as success that you can achieve. From a business point of view, you will acquire fame and will get everything you need to turn it into something beautiful. Your work is appreciated and the desire for more only increases. It is a work card that represents your professional life. When "The Scythe" is also present, it points to a departure. Surrounding love cards speak of a loved one at work. "The Ring" close to this card refers to business cooperation with the partner.

Card 46 • The Railroad
Playing Card • Two of clubs
Keywords • Journey, city trip, getaway, an accident

"The Railroad" represents a long and distant journey, a trip or just a nice weekend away. If "The Broken Glass" is there, then we must pay attention on the road: excessive speed, driving under the influence, or unforeseen obstacles. An accident is not far away. Surrounded by love cards, you will set out on a journey with your loved one. In the presence of work cards, you will travel abroad for work.

Card 47 • The Bride
Playing Card • King of spades
Keywords • Single woman, goals, turbulence

"The Bride" is a single lady who passionately pursues her goals. It's a lady who likes to live her life independantly. In addition to this standard meaning, "The Bride" also symbolizes our current relationship. When this card falls close to love cards, we are in a turbulent relationship and problems must be solved. "The Bride" is a lonely lady who lives primarily in her own emotional world, and who has difficulties expressing those emotions. If "The Bride" is surrounded by positive cards such as "Amor" or "The Order," all is well in the relationship.

Card 48 • The Money Safe
Playing Card • Three of diamonds
Keywords • Money, wealth

"The Money Safe" shows money and wealth, and by extension everything that is important for you to live a rich life. If the closed door is facing the person card, there is a loss of money due to speculation (or institutions pulling back, rejection of certain subsidies, repayments of loans, etc.). With the open side of "The Money Safe" toward the person card, you can expect profits that are entirely favorable. Here too, we examine the cards surrounding "The Money Safe." When the closed door of "The Money Safe" is near "The Amor" card, it means that it's not wise to continue to support your partner financially.

Card 49 • The Eye
Playing Card • Four of spades
Keywords • interest, friends, spying

"The Eye" is a positive card and shows us the interest that friends have in us. If this card is far away from the person card, then we will be spied on by our friends. "The Eye" sees everything, both the beautiful and the difficult things. Yet it is a predominantly positive card. In relationships, it points out that there are no secrets between both partners and that they can communicate openly. When "The Mice" or "The Book" fall near this card, it is recommended that the partners improve their mutual communication.

Card 50 • The Bear
Playing Card • King of clubs
Keywords • Power, control, dominance

"The Bear" represents a strong personality, capable of dominating the querent and convincing them that he is right. It is someone who wants to exercise control over everything and everyone and plays a power game in that sense. Don't fall for this. Near money cards "The Bear" can also mean successful investments.

Card 51 • The Lion
Playing Card • Six of diamonds
Keywords • Bad news, shock

"The Lion" brings bad news that is shocking in nature regardless of whether it's a love, work or financial message. The surrounding cards determine where this ominous message will be coming from. If we see "The Flowers" e.g., then the feelings are no longer what they should be and that is the cause of the terrible news.

Card 52 • The Shepherd
Playing Card • Jack of spades
Keywords • Intense love, sincere affection

"The Shepherd" is a positive card that indicates that our partner loves us sincerely and intensely. "The Shepherd" is not only loving in his relationship, but also outside of it. He is compassionate and respectful towards his fellow man. Wherever this card falls, it always brings a positive outcome that we don't have to worry about.

Working with the Joker

The Joker serves to give a simple yes/no answer to a question or wish. Before you start, remove the two person cards from the deck. The question must be asked very specifically. Shuffle the cards while you focus on the question or wish. When the cards have been sufficiently shuffled, deal the cards face up and one at a time into a pile, counting aloud.

If the Joker appears as an even number, the answer is yes. If it falls on an odd number, the answer is no. If the answer is no, look at the three to four previous cards to find out why the question was answered unfavorably.

Example

You are dealing the cards and at position 16 the Joker appears. This is a yes to the question of the querent in question.

Suppose the Joker comes out at position 27, this is an unfavorable answer. We should have a look at the three to four previous cards, in order to find out why the answer was negative. Consider card images as well as playing card inserts.

Example

Suppose someone wants to know if they will keep their job. The Joker appears at position 27 (odd) and the four preceding cards are as follows:

Card 13: "The Snake"
Card 31: "The Roads"
Card 26: "The Park"
Card 4: "The Key"

This combination indicates failures at work and people who are not always sincere towards the querent ("The Snake"). The querent feels so uncomfortable with this that she makes the decision herself and quits her job ("The Roads"). She goes looking for something else that makes her feel better (the sun on the side of "The Roads" touches the card of "The Park"). This new job offers her the solution ("The Key") to be happy again.

4
The Different Spreads

Getting started

Closely examine all the cards: what impressions do you get? Which images do you like? What kind of feeling do you get from the playing card inserts?

As a card reader, I think it's important to make your own associations, in addition to the knowledge you gain from this book while practicing. This means that you let your thoughts, emotions and intuition run free without being afraid to make mistakes. By doing this, you will gradually acquire multiple associations and you will get a better and more coherent story.

Starting may seem difficult, but once you understand the basics, it will become second nature.

Before we get started, we first ask ourselves the following questions:

- Which kind of spread are we using?
- Does the querent want a full picture of the future or rather an insight into a specific existing situation?
- Do we opt for a Grand Tableau?
- Or do we prefer a themed reading?

These questions are extremely important. After all, not everyone wants a complete overview of the future. In my daily work I always experience quite a diversity of expectations. Some people only want to know something about a relationship, while others are only interested in work. Who am I to reveal a complete picture of the future in that case? It is an approach that works great for me and it's also the fairest and purest way of working.

I will give some illustrated examples of spreads, so that you can link the type of question and the method that I used.

Short spreads with past, present and future

We take the person card (card 18, if the querent is a woman and card 19, if the querent is a man) and put it in position 1. Shuffle and fan the cards. The querent now draws six cards, which you then lay out according to the following example:

Card 1 = the person card   **Card 2 + 6** = past

Card 3 + 5 = present   **Card 4 + 7** = near future

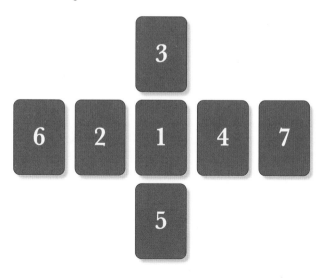

A lady asks if she can expect a love relationship to come her way in the near future. These are the cards that she pulled:

In the past we have cards 28 "The Anchor" and 27 "The Dog." This tells us that the lady is a faithful and loyal person.

In the present we see cards 51 "The Lion" and 41 "The Roses." This indicates that the lady has experienced quite a few disappointments ("The Lion") and went through a lot in the past. **If we read "The Lion" diagonally with "The Dog,"** it shows us that her trust was betrayed because she was too good and too naive towards others. She needs to learn to take a wait-and-see approach in some cases.

"The Roses" tell us that she is insecure: someone who is deeply concerned about her appearance and uncertain about it. "The Dog" + "The Roses" + "The Lion": she is uncertain in one way or another, so she always wants to look her best.

In the near future we see cards 38 "The Flames" and 7 "The Flowers." This combination indicates that she will continue to do everything she can to pursue her happiness, despite the negative experiences from her recent past. She is also appreciated for who she is, so there is no need to be insecure about her appearance ("The Roses" + "The Flames"). Will she bump into someone? There will be contacts that she will be able to build upon. These contacts are currently still in the friendship zone ("The Anchor" + "The Dog" + "The Lady" + "The Flames" + "The Flowers").

The playing card inserts

There is a majority of **Diamonds**. Above her head we see "The Lion," the six of diamonds. She is worried about her financial situation. We can predict a financial improvement based on the other diamonds. Still, she needs to be careful with her resources, because nine of spades ("The Roses") speaks of overspending.

Conclusion: it is a predominantly positive spread.

The Star Spread examines five cards around a situation card.

First, look for the corresponding situation or theme card in the deck. To clarify a love issue, take card 42 "Amor." For a question about a child, separate card 12, "The Children," and so on. Place this card in the middle, as this will be your situation or theme card. After the cards have been shuffled and spread out, ask the querent to draw five cards and lay them out according to the star-shaped pattern below.

This method paints a short but powerful picture of how someone is handling a certain situation. It also shows you how a specific situation can evolve in the short term (three months).

Card 1: This shows the stumbling blocks that influence the outcome of card 5.

Card 2 + card 3: These are karma or fate cards. This means that the situations are unavoidable for the person asking the question. They serve as a warning for what is about to come. It's a life lesson that they will have to face in order to be stronger in the future. Thanks to this lesson, the querent will not make the same mistake again in the future.

Card 4: Represents the near future. What is the querent going to do with the life lessons in cards 2 and 3? This can still be adjusted, as long as we remember what fate still needs to bring.

Card 5: The result or the outcome.

A lady wants to know how her current relationship will develop. We get the following spread:

At position 1, the stumbling blocks in the relationship, we see card 50 "The Bear" as an answer to the specific question from our lady. The playing card insert shows a king of clubs, so in this case her partner. When we zoom in on the stumbling blocks, we see a man who exerts a lot of power and control in the relationship. He is quite dominant and always wants to be right. The message is that the lady should not accept this situation.

Position 2 and 3, the karma or fate of their relationship, shows us "The Snake" and "The Heart." Because "The Snake" is above "The Bear" (the lady's partner), this refers to his toxic and unhealthy way of asserting control. "The Snake" in the karma line indicates that there is some work to be done about his behavior. It exhausts the lady considerably. "The Heart" nevertheless shows a very intense love between the two and since "The Heart" neutralizes negative cards, it also neutralizes the negative influence of "The Snake." This does not immediately resolve the problems, but the partner is willing to work on them.

Position 4 gives a glimpse of the near future. "The Stork" here indicates changes. In this question "The Stork" doesn't necessarily refer to a move, but points to changes in the relationship. Changes that are necessary to maintain the relationship. Ultimately, a positive change will occur. Positive, because this is what the result card is showing us. The partner will address his dominant character.

Position 5 as outcome. "The Pig," as an answer to the lady's question, is a symbol of happiness and abundance. They would love to stay together, which will also be the case. This card promises a pleasant outcome, provided that the cards in positions 2 and 3 are considered.

The Relationship Method

In the relationship method, we remove both person cards from the deck: card number 18 "The Lady" and card number 19 "The Gentleman."

We place "The Gentleman" on the left of the spread, "The Lady" on the right.

We shuffle and fan the cards. Finally, we let the querent draw eight cards that we reveal according to the method below.

Cards 1, 2 and 3 under "The Gentleman" show how the man experiences the relationship.

Cards 4, 5 and 6 under "The Lady" show how the lady relates to the man.

Card 7 shows the obstacles or stumbling blocks between both parties.

Card 8, the bonus card, gives advice. What can be done to improve the relationship? What is needed to achieve this?

From card 7 we consider both the card image and the playing card symbol. The playing card symbol explains the stumbling blocks.

From card 8, the bonus card, we also take the playing card symbol into account, and combine it with the one from card 7, the obstacle.

In this spread it is again important to recognize connections. Try to evaluate as many combinations as possible as this will enable you to get more details.

Example:

Read the cards for a man on page 64, along with those of the lady (1 and 4, 2 and 5, 3 and 6).

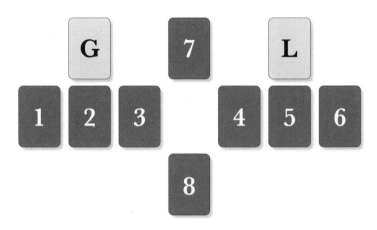

Let's have a look at a detailed example of a relationship reading:

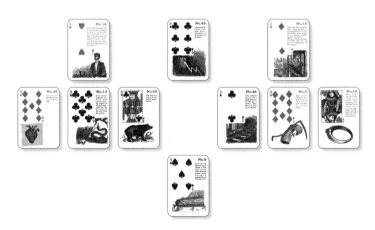

**Under "The Gentleman," we find "The Heart,"
"The Snake" and "The Bear."** This shows us that,
regardless of the situation, the love of the man for the
woman is real, it is a love with strong and deep feelings.
"The Snake," on the other hand, shows the destructive
side of the man—the man suffers from negative energy. In
combination with "The Bear" we observe a compulsive and
unhealthy way of controlling and dominating. "The Snake"
is a toxic person and "The Bear" is overbearing. The lady
must pay attention to this.

**Under the person card of the woman, we see "The
Railroad," "The Scythe" and "The Ring."** "The Railroad" and "The Scythe" show us that the lady will be facing
a decision. Will she end the relationship? "The Scythe" and
"The Ring" indicate that her partner's behavior will become
unbearable, which will make her want to break up with him.

**Card 7, the obstacle between both people is "The
Lightning."** This card predicts unpleasant surprises, things
the lady hadn't expected at all. In this example, this man-
ifests as recurring conflicts that are constantly unleashing
arguments.

Card 8, the bonus card, is "The Coffin." This card
shows us the final outcome. An abrupt end to the relationship is on the horizon. These two people won't stay together
because of their destructive patterns. The card "The Railroad" is on the lady's side of the spread, so it is she who
ultimately makes the decision to end the relationship.

If we take a closer look at the playing card inserts, we can
see that the man has a majority of clubs. This points to fear,

miscommunication and especially to conflict. The foundation of their relationship has completely disappeared. There is no longer peace and stability.

The lady has mostly red cards, namely the hearts and the diamonds. This indicates that her emotions are damaged and that she isn't happy with her partner anymore. The five of spades in turn points to a blockage that is present with both people. For the man, this means that his fears are troubling him, the lady in turn realizes that her feelings for him are seriously falling short.

Cross Spread with Obstacles consisting of 24 cards

This spread is perfect when we want to evaluate an existing situation or as an additional spread next to a Grand Tableau. We use 24 cards for this method. Here we proceed as we did with the other spreads: shuffle, fan, and then ask the querent to draw 24 cards. Finally, we lay out the cards according to the diagram on the following page.

Cards 1-12 in the cross represent the karma or fate of the querent.

Cards 13-24 (underneath and above the cross) show us the obstacles and external influences. The following example will clarify this:

Cards 9, 5 and 1 represent the recent past

Cards 3, 7 and 11 show the present or what is about to happen

Cards 2, 6 and 10 talk about the near future

Cards 4, 8 and 12 also represent the present

Cards 13, 14, 15, 16, 17 and 18 (the six cards above the person card) show us the obstacles or stumbling blocks that the querent needs to overcome. They are inevitable.

Cards 19, 20, 21, 22, 23 and 24 (the six cards underneath the person card) indicate what is needed, what needs to be done or what requires attention to improve the future.

Cards 15, 11 and 16 are read together

Cards 22, 12 and 21 are read together

With this method, it's also important to notice connections. Dare to be bold and make all kinds of combinations. And yes, combinations that come to you intuitively during the reading are more than welcome.

In this example, the male querent wants to find out how his relationship life will evolve. Thanks to this layout we achieve a beautiful and clear story. You can read how to do this on the following pages.

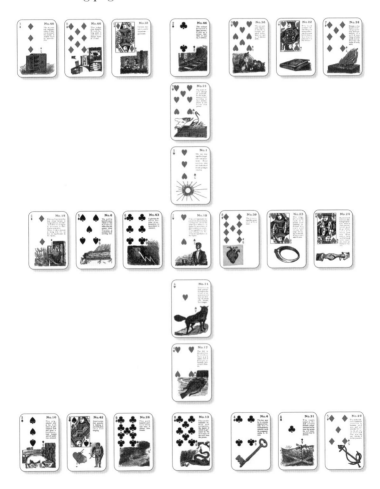

Cards 9, 5 and 1 show the past. Here we can clearly see that the man had a previous relationship that didn't turn out well ("The Lightning"). The relationship was suddenly ended by the lady (card 18).

Cards 3, 7, 11, 4, 8 and 12 show us what is going on in the present "The Railroad," "The Stork" and "The Sun" above the male person card explain that despite the sorrows of the past, positive and beautiful changes are finally on the way. He will withdraw a little and just take a time out, which he needs to get back on his feet. Under the person card we see "The Fox," "The Fish" and "The Snake." With these cards, it is advisable for the querent to be careful in the coming period not to engage with negative people who want to take advantage of him, especially financially. This is a wealthy man and "The Snake" + "The Fox" indicate that people might take advantage of this.

Cards 2, 6 and 10 give us a glimpse of the near future "The Heart," "The Ring" and "Hand in Hand." This hints to an encounter with a lady (Queen of hearts), that might lead to a relationship.

It will be a lady he can trust ("Hand in Hand"). However, he must make sure not to end up in the same situation as before. Because the cards in the cross are warning us that certain patterns could repeat themselves in the future.

Cards 13, 14, 15, 16, 17 and 18 represent obstacles: We find "The Money Safe," "Broken Glass" and "The Children" at the top left corner. These cards indicate that the querent must be careful not to become a victim of his wealth. He is advised to temper his good-natured attitude a little, and not to be too naive ("The Children"). He should be more careful with his money instead of giving it away. Giving it away means that he will never see it again ("The Broken Glass").

The cards on the right, namely 16, 17 and 18, illustrate that this man knows his indulgence is a stumbling block. He will come to realize that he needs to correct this ("The Book"). "The Flames," in turn, provide positive reinforcement, which means that he has learned his lesson now and that he will be less haughty and stubborn ("The Cat") in the future.

Cards 19, 20, 21, 22, 23 and 24 indicate what he can do to positively influence his future.

Here we see "The Key," "The Roads" and "The Anchor" at the bottom right. There will be important changes to his attitude towards life, which he himself will actively implement in order not to fall into old patterns. The clubs dominate, which means that he is finally able to let go of his fears. He no longer must prove himself by chasing after money and status. The querent will therefore improve his attitude towards life ("The Anchor" in combination with the Five of diamonds).

The cards at the bottom left, namely "The Pig," "Amor" and "The Park," promise a positive trend for the future. It is time to bring some form of renewal into his life and make new social contacts. However, the spades dominate here, indicating that he feels somewhat inhibited about mingling with other people. But the Queen of spades (card of the lover) announces that a new partner will soon accompany him.

Traditional Gypsy Spread with 17 Cards

For this traditional Gypsy Spread we no longer make a distinction between past, present or future. We do examine what is happening around the person and what the outside influences are, also called karma or fate.

The person cards are not used in this reading. We will read the cards starting from the first one, the significator. The two cards to the right of the significator (cards 4 + 2) show the result.

Shuffle the cards and fan them out. The querent then draws 17 cards, after which you lay them out according to the following pattern.

Inner square = what is active around the person
Outer square = near and distant future

Remember: Both squares influence each other and determine the final result. That's why it is important to carefully read the diagonal, horizontal and vertical lines and to go through both squares together.

First, we start with the inner square. This square has a direct impact on the querent, since it tells you a bit more about what is going on in their life right now. What prevails here? The clubs, hearts, diamonds or spades? Are the card images positive or rather negative?

After this we focus on the outer square. What is coming their way? Here we also consider playing card inserts and card images. What prevails here?

In addition to the method described previously, the cards can also be read as follows:

Cards 1 + 7 + 1 + 9 + 5 can be read diagonally.
Cards 7 + 6 + 1 + 8 + 3 can be read diagonally.

Cards 6 + 2 + 1 + 4 + 2 can be read horizontally.
Cards 8 + 3 + 1 + 5 + 4 can be read vertically.

And so on.

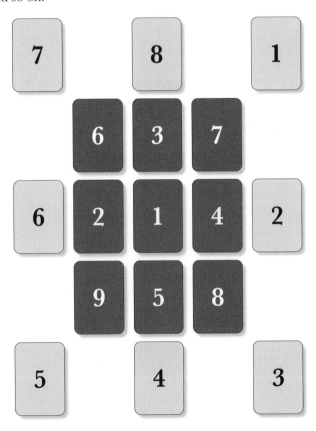

In the spread below we can see the cards that came up:

The significator card is "Amor" (Queen of spades).
This is where we start the reading. We are dealing with a
bitter lady who is very emotional and struggles to filter her
emotions (mostly hearts around the significator). On the
other hand, it also means that we are dealing with a very

sensitive person. "The Sun," "The House" and "The Fish" tell us that this lady is nevertheless successful in life and has no financial concerns. We note that she is a hard worker, who always delves into new things, eager to widen her horizons ("The Book" + "The Moon +" The Sun "). She likes to be seen by her environment ("The Fish" + "Hand in Hand" + "The Flowers"). "The Clover" in turn shows us two things. First, her own feelings and emotions are honest and genuine. Secondly, she aspires to a stable life without sudden changes, especially on a professional level ("The Moon" + "The Clover" + " The Flowers"). She is a perfectionist, who does everything she can to bring matters to a successful conclusion.

The outer square consists of "The Clouds," "The Mice" and "Broken Glass." In the future she needs to watch out for emotional complications ("The Clouds") with regards to a future partner (significator card). She is being warned for impending discord. "The Mice" protect her from the emotional pain that she might experience as a result of her injured pride ("The Mice" + "The Heart" + the heart suits under "The Mice"). She also needs to ensure that her relationship troubles don't affect her work, as this could lead to financial losses ("Broken Glass" + "The Fish" + "Amor" + "The Moon" = diagonal).

"The Tower" and "The Coffin" point to blockages. The lady is fighting an inner battle. She is too trusting ("Hand in Hand" + "The Coffin"). It would be better if she could distance herself from certain people. However, due to her sensitive nature, she is easily carried away and she no longer has an eye for possible negative aspects. "The Fox," "The Bear" and "The Mountain" confirm the rest of the outer square: she must be careful who she allows into her life. She will be directly confronted with false and unreliable people in her work environment ("The Fox" + "The Moon" + "The Bear"). But...fortunately "The Mountain" shows her that she will overcome her problems. She will throw all her resources into the battle to achieve this. Furthermore, "The Bear" + "The Mountain" point to an individual who wants to gain power over her.

"Hand In Hand" and "The Coffin" next to the significator show us that she wants to quit her current job. Thanks to this decision she will find more inner peace. It is very likely that she will be able to work from home, possibly by becoming self-employed ("The House" + "The Fish" + "Hand in Hand").

Exercise

You can get much more out of this spread. It's important to practice a lot on your own and to associate freely. Try to read the diagonal lines in this spread. Write down all your impressions. Start with the keywords and expand, so that you create a unique story.

Notes

Grand Tableau with 52 cards according to the Gypsy method

This method involves a complete spread with all 52 cards. The Grand Tableau is extremely suitable when you want to get a total picture of the querent's life. This method really shows us everything. However, a thorough knowledge of the card meanings and previous spreads is required before you begin to use this spread.

We proceed as follows: we remove all jokers from the deck, as well as the person cards. If you lay the cards for a man, place the person card with number 19 (Two of hearts) in the position as shown in the illustration on page 74 and put the Lady card back in the deck. Follow the same steps the other way around for a female querent.

After you have given the cards a good shuffle, lay them out from left to right. Start with one row of six cards and continue with two rows of eight cards. In the fourth row place three cards, then the person card of the man or woman, and then complete the same row with four cards. Lay another two rows of eight cards and then complete our Grand Tableau with six cards at the bottom.

The Grand Tableau Spread should look like this:

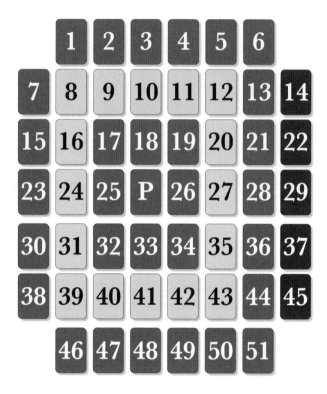

How do we read this spread? Well, the principle is the same as the extended method with seventeen cards. To outline it easily and clearly, I have marked the different positions in various shades of gray. This will make it easier to see what you are going to read first.

As a beginner, we consider all the squares separately to avoid the risk of confusion.

Remember: The farther removed a card is from the person card, the longer it takes to exerts its influence. The closer to the person card, the quicker its meaning will manifest itself.

The five cards on the far right, the cards 14, 22, 29, 37 and 45, represent the final result. The answer to the question can be found here.

Cards 17, 18, 19, 26, 34, and 33, 32 and 25 indicate what is hanging over the querent's head: karma and fate. What is going on in their head, what are they worried about? What playing card suits are predominant here? Are the card images mainly positive or negative?

We start with the inner square: What do you see around the person card? Start with card 17 and continue clockwise to card 25. This square explains what the person is dealing with.

We check if there is a preponderance of certain suits. When nothing jumps out, you don't have to interpret the playing card inserts yet. You can do that later, when you start reading the diagonals and the other squares.

It's important to always work from the inside out. So, work from the person card to the first square, then continue to the outer square. Only as the very last step read the diagonals.

As soon as you have analyzed the first eight cards around the person card, as illustrated in the following example, move to the next step.

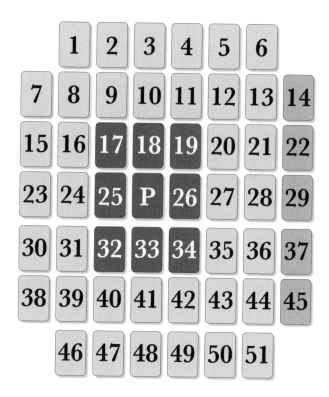

Next we zoom in on the second square. We begin at the card in position 8 and continue to the card at position 12. We first read: 8, 9, 10, 11 and 12.

Then we read: 12, 20, 27, 35, 43.

We continue to: 43, 42, 41, 40 and 39.

Finally, we look at: 39, 31, 24, 16 and 8.

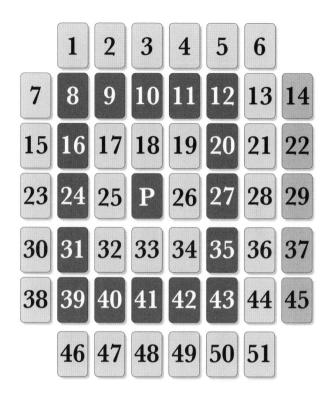

Examine all the cards: are there predominantly positive or negative cards? What do the playing card inserts say? In the beginning of the book you will find a clear description of the different suits.

Follow the steps as described above. All these cards describe the external influences and what will inevitably happen to the querent. They give further meaning to cards 17, 18, 19, 26, 34, 33, 32 and 25 (inner square).

We will now read the outer square.

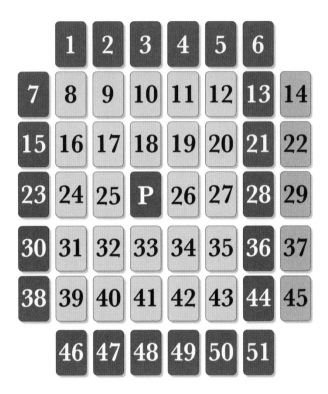

Here we start with card number 1 and end with card number 6.

Next, we will read cards 6 to 51. We continue from 51 to 46.

Finally, we read cards 38 to 7.

The outer frame gives us insight into the future of the querent. Both the images and playing card inserts are taken into consideration.

You can combine the cards as follows:

1 + 2 6 + 13   3 + 4 21 + 28

5 + 6   36 + 44 And so on

Once you have a good understanding of the cards and the other spreads, you can learn to combine several cards such as:

1 + 2 + 3 + 4
6 + 13 + 21 + 28
44 + 51 + 50 + 49 And so on

Cards 8, 9, 10, 11, 12, 20, 27, 35, 43, 42, 41, 40, 39, 31, 24 and 16 indicate what the querant can expect to happen with certainty in the coming six months. Things to pay attention to but also action that will need to be taken.

Cards 1, 2, 3, 4, 5, 6, 13, 21, 28, 36, 44, 51, 50, 49, 48, 47, 46, 38, 30, 23, 15 and 7 represent the distant future, up to a maximum of two years. Here you can unravel important and detailed issues. Take note of the connections between the cards.

As previously mentioned, cards 14, 22, 29, 37 and 45 show us the final outcome.

In this spread we will also read the diagonal lines. Every square around the person card influences a different square. We read the diagonal lines as follows, starting with the person card:

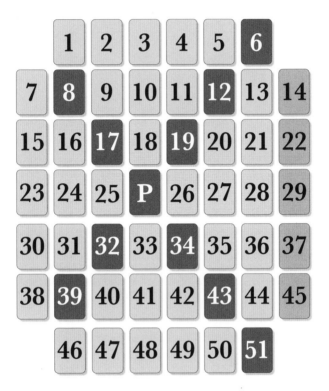

We also include the straight lines around the person card (see image on page 81). Here we make a distinction between past, present and future.

The left represents the past.

Above the person card we see the present or what is hanging over their head.

The right represents the future. The further to the right the card is from the person card, the later the card will have its effect in the future. Under the person card we read again the present and what the querent must take into account.

Have a look at the following example:

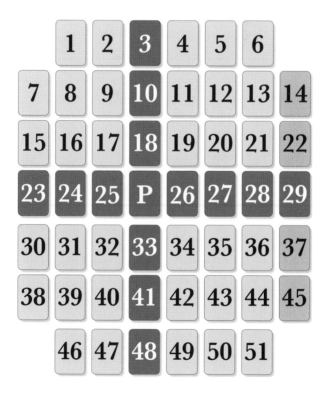

We read the past as follows: cards 23, 24 and 25. The present, above and below: cards 3, 10, 18, 33, 41 and 48.

The future is shown by the cards: 26, 27, 28 and 29.

We can also consider the first four cards around the person card, in particular cards 25, 18, 26 and 33. This will tell you what things from the past (card 25) influence the future (card 26), and what in turn influences the present (card 33).

We go one step further and read the squares from both top left and bottom and top right and bottom.

The top and bottom squares to the left represent the person's past. Have they already let go of the past? Are they still encountering obstacles that affect the future and the present?

The top and bottom squares to the right give more details about what is going to happen in the future. The example on page 84 will make this clear.

Squares representing the past

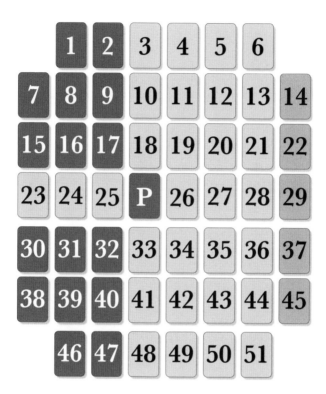

This is how we read the diagonal lines of the past:

Cards 8 + 17   Cards 31 + 40

Cards 7 + 16   Cards 30 + 39 + 47

Cards 15 + 8 + 2   Cards 38 + 46

Cards 1 + 9

Squares representing the future

1	2	3	4	5	6	
7	8	9	10	11	12	13	14
15	16	17	18	19	20	21	22
23	24	25	P	26	27	28	29
30	31	32	33	34	35	36	37
38	39	40	41	42	43	44	45
46	47	48	49	50	51	

The diagonal lines for the future are:

Cards 20 + 13   Cards 35 + 44

Cards 21 + 14   Cards 42 + 50

Cards 19 + 12 + 6   Cards 36 + 45

Cards 4 + 12 + 21   Cards 34 + 43 + 51

                       Cards 49 + 43 + 36

Does the querent want an answer to a love question? In that case we look for the "Love" card in the Grand Tableau. We then consider the cards that are immediately around it. The cards around "Amor" (card 42) serve as connection cards:

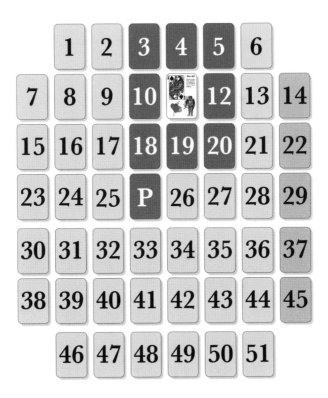

Then consider the card on the left at position 10 (near past). Cards 9, 8 and 7 also provide additional information about what has happened in the past in the love life of the querent.

Cards 3, 4 and 5 represent the things that will happen in the love life of the querent. The card on position 12 on the right-hand side (near future) shows you what the querent can expect to happen soon. Cards 13 and 14 (distant future) show us further developments, i.e. what can be expected in the distant future with regards to the love life.

The diagonals around "Amor" give more details on the person and how they view the relationship.

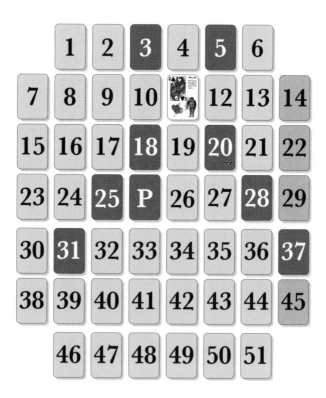

Cards 18, 25 and 31 represent the past and show us how they influence the current question about love. Are they positive cards and what do the playing card inserts tell you?

Cards 20, 28 and 37 shed light on the future with regards to the question about love. What can the querent expect and what should they pay attention to? Here, we also consider the playing card inserts in addition to the card images.

Cards 3 and 5 indicate what the stumbling blocks are regarding the question about love. If position 3 is "The Fox" and position 5 is "Hand in Hand," we can state that the querent is having trust issues. An analysis of the whole picture can show us why.

The five outer cards (see next page) show the outcome and formulate an opinion at the same time. The outcome does not have to be inevitable. Rather, the advice outlines what the person can do to see other questions answered.

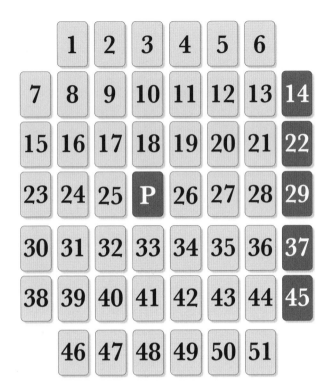

Cards 14, 22, 29, 37 and 45 provide the result or give us advice. Let us assume that the following cards have been dealt in these positions:

14 "The Park"
22 "The Roads"
29 "The Pig"
37 "The Anchor"
45 "The Sun"

The querent must be more open towards the future. They can no longer stay stuck in their emotional world ("The Park" + "The Roads" + "The Pig"). As a matter of fact, it would serve them well to make new contacts and forge friendships. Because happiness doesn't just come knocking at your door! Stepping out of social isolation is the message (the clubs dominate) that you can give the querent. If they succeed, they can soon look forward to an abundance of love and happiness ("The Anchor" + "The Sun").

5
An Overview of
the 52 Gypsy Cards

To make things easier, all the cards are listed below so that you can immediately see which are positive, negative or neutral.

Positive cards	Neutral cards	Negative cards
The Sun	The Children	The Coffin
The Moon	The Rider	The Scythe
The House	The Ship	The Birds
The Key	The Lady	The Fox
The Tree	The Gentleman	The Snake
The Flowers	The Stork	The Book
The Pig	The Roads	The Clouds
The Letter	The Cat	The Mice
The Fish	The Railroad	The Rod
The Lily	The Bride	The Mountain
The Ring	The Money Safe	The Tower
Hand in Hand	The Eye	The Rapiers
The Park		The Lightning
The Dog		The Broken Glass
The Anchor		The Bear
The Clover		The Lion
The Star		
The Flames		
The Heart		
The Wine		
The Roses		
Amor		
The Order		
The Shepherd		

6
A Closer Look at
the Person Cards

In the Gypsy card system, a distinction is made between different categories of person cards. The Romani have divided these person cards into youngsters (jacks), ladies (queens) and men (kings). These always have a specific meaning in the spread, and they all have their own specific characteristics, which we will discuss in detail in this section.

Card 14 Jack of diamonds

This is a young character who is very ambitious in life and has a strong business sense. Negotiating runs through his blood. In emotional matters he is not really on the ball and is rather hesitant.

He doesn't seem to know what he wants. In real life, he can represent both a male and female person.

Card 22 Jack of hearts

The Jack of hearts is a young person who is sensitive and introverted. He is shy and prefers to stay in his own emotional world. These people need structure and quickly experience emotional instability when confronted with setbacks. They also tend to get discouraged faster. The Jack of hearts usually means well and has a big heart. According to the Romani, the Jack of hearts represents a male person in real life.

Card 45 Jack of clubs

This is a young character who will do everything he can to reach his goal. He is quite ambitious in life and wants to do things his way without considering other people. He comes across as controlling and overbearing and shows no mercy (the suit of clubs represents discord).

Card 52 Jack of spades

The Jack of spades is a young man who stands up for himself. Don't step on his toes because then he becomes resentful. He can be dominant and opportunistic. This jack knows what he wants and is a go-getter. If you respect him, he will respect you in return. He loves innovation and is adventurous. According to the Romani the Jack of spades is a male person.

Card 12 Queen of diamonds

The Queen of diamonds is a prosperous and enterprising woman who knows what she wants. She has strong business acumen and is a great professional counselor. She is valued by everyone and knows how to run a company. The Queen of diamonds will listen to other people's ideas but in the end, she stays true to her own vision. Furthermore, this lady acts very intuitively, which can cause her to get lost sometimes.

Card 23 Queen of hearts

The Queen of hearts is an emotional being. She likes to take care of other people but often gets too caught up doing so and tends to lose herself by putting others first. She doesn't realize that her self-sacrifice can turn against her. Yet she can come across as frivolous, but this is often just a way of covering up disappointment. She is kind-hearted and symbolizes a mother figure according to the Romani.

Card 40 Queen of clubs

This lady either loves you or hates you. She is smart, cunning and can get envious. She likes to choose her followers and does everything she can to manipulate them. The Queen of clubs loves the spotlight and is not afraid of gossip. According to the Romani the suit of clubs is not exactly a positive one so it's better to avoid this lady if you don't like these character traits.

Card 42 Queen of spades

The Queen of spades is a lonely character who is embittered by life. She tends to isolate herself socially, which in turn gives rise to a solitary existence. She is afraid to commit to friendships and romantic relationships. She has a lot to offer to a partner, but she must first say goodbye to her self-imposed loneliness.

According to the Romani, the Queen of spades is a wealthy person, but loneliness can put a heavy weight on her happiness in life.

Card 15 King of diamonds

The King of diamonds knows what he wants. He is self-assured and tends to exert his will. He understands the art of turning little into plenty. This king likes to go out to investigate all the possibilities, and he often succeeds in his undertakings. He is verbally strong and according to the Romani he will often work as a sales representative in real life. He has a way with words. "Doing business" is second nature to this man.

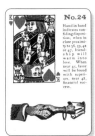

Card 24 King of hearts

The King of hearts is a reliable character you can always count on. He's a father figure and represents a good friend or life partner. Just like the Queen of hearts, he tends to put himself second to others. His patience is infinite and that can sometimes be to his disadvantage. He is a sensitive man and family ties are very important to him. According to the Romani, the King of hearts can represent a father, a good friend or a partner.

Card 50 King of clubs

This is a righteous man with both feet on the ground. He is very wise, and you can always count on him to give you honest and sincere advice. He can sometimes come across as tough, but he never means bad. According to the Romani, this King of clubs stands for our own father, father-in-law or father figure who we can always count on.

Card 47 King of spades

The King of spades is a versatile man who is very knowledgeable. He likes to delve into different subjects and loves to philosophize. He is strict and is quick to judge. Furthermore, these gentlemen are wise and like to show authority and power. These men are emotionally difficult to reach because of their strict and rather surly manner. According to the Romani the King of spades is a brother, a counselor, a father or father-in-law.

Reading the person cards

As discussed in detail at the beginning of the book, reading the playing card inserts is just as important as reading the person cards. Taking the playing cards into account will allow you to get more details out of the spread. Below we will show a few examples in which the person cards are read.

Suppose your querent asks you if they will meet someone. You have decided to do a Grand Tableau so you will look for the theme card, in this case card 39 "The Heart."

52 THE SHEPHERD (Jack of spades)
39 THE HEART   45 THE ORDER (Jack of clubs)
15 THE LETTER (King of diamonds)

The cards above the theme card and the first card to the right of the theme card represent their personality. In the example above, those are the Jack of spades (top) and the Jack of clubs (right).

First, the jacks have the upper hand, so we are undoubtedly dealing with a young man. If we want to find out more about his personality, we first need to read the playing card inserts separately (spades and clubs).

Next, we zoom in on the personality traits associated with the Jack of spades and the Jack of clubs.

The example above shows us a young man who is standing his ground. Don't step on his toes, because he could get rather aggressive. He is a dominant go-getter who knows exactly what he wants. If you respect him, it will be mutual. Furthermore, he is always looking for innovation. The spades point to a young man who tends to encounter obstacles because he is driven by fear and tends to hold on to certain things.

The first card that falls next to the theme card is the Jack of clubs. This is a young character who will do everything he can to reach his goals. He can be ruthless in this sense.

This person is ambitious in life and all too often things must be done his way, without any consideration for the people around him. He comes across as domineering in the way he talks and acts and wants to maintain control over everything he does. The suit of clubs in turn represent discord.

Another example:

Someone asks you if his girlfriend can be trusted. In the Grand Tableau you look for "The Dog," card number 27. The example below will briefly illustrate the method.

13 THE SNAKE (Eight of clubs)
27 THE DOG   40 THE WINE (Queen of clubs)
35 THE TOWER (Ten of clubs)

The clubs have the upper hand here, and the images of cards 13 and 10 are not so positive either. With the placement of the Queen of clubs to the right of the theme card, we can conclude the following: it's a shrewd and cunning lady who is either for or against you. She likes to be in the spotlight and has jealous tendencies.

When analyzing the playing card inserts of card 13 and card 35, you will see that these are pointing to discord. The advice to the querent is that it would be better to avoid this person. She is not always sincere, and the world only revolves around her. Is she a sincere friend? No, not entirely.

This is how you can interpret all the people cards, based on their character traits and the information that you get from the suits and card images. Look for dominating influences and ask yourself what would give a positive or negative outcome.

When doing this type of spread, it's important to explain the technique to the querent rather than just trying to construct a 'beautiful' story. The above example does not necessarily mean that the querent and the lady in question cannot come together to form a relationship. However, both jacks point to dominance and it's not easy to deal with that in a relationship. What the querent does with this information depends on their free will and is a decision they need to make.

7
Card Combinations

In this chapter you will find different card combinations that will help you when you are practicing.

If you are at the beginning of your Gypsy card journey and still find it difficult to interpret certain spreads, this section will help you to obtain effective answers.

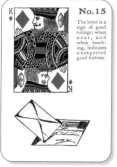

Card 1 • The Sun

+ The Moon = popularity and happiness at work
+ The House = happiness and success in all your undertakings
+ The Key = solutions coming into sight
+ The Flowers = positive and genuine feelings
+ The Tree = wishes are fulfilled
+ The Fox = you find out who you can or cannot trust
+ The Rider = you can expect positive news
+ The Rider + The Snake + The Tower = disagreements will arise
+ The Stork + Hand in Hand + The Ring = a love situation that brings about a positive change

Card 2 • The Moon

+ The Rider = messages about work
+ The Snake = watch out for dishonesty at work
+ The Fox = unreliable people at work
+ The House = a business from home
+ The Key = insights regarding work
+ The Book = getting to know things at work
+ The Clouds = conflicts at work
+ The Rod + The Mountain = disagreements and miscommunication with a colleague

Card 3 • The House

+ Amor = marriage
+ The Stork = relocation or a change in the current home
+ The Tree = feeling good at home
+ The Fox + The Dog = pay attention to who you are dealing with
+ The Mice = loss or theft at home
+ The Mice + The Fish = stolen funds
+ The Book + The Clouds = secrets cause separation or distance

Card 4 • The Key

+ The Broken Glass = there is no solution
+ The Broken Glass + The Lightning = irreversible break-up
+ The Fish = financial solution
+ The Order = appreciation
+ The Railroad = taking a break
+ The Shepherd = intense and genuine feelings

Card 5 • The Tree

+ The Roses = too busy with looks
+ The Mice = loss of self-esteem
+ The Tower = blocked feelings
+ The Scythe + The Coffin = poor health
+ The Dog + The Birds + The Snake = watch out for gossip
+ The Children = watch out for naivety
+ The Heart + The Anchor = a stable love relationship

Card 6 • The Coffin

+ The Heart = the sudden end of the relationship
+ The Ring = the sudden end of a marriage
+ The Moon = the sudden end of a job
+ The Dog = the end of a friendship
+ The Lily = worries and moral quandries in the family circle
+ The Park = social isolation, not going out and closing
  oneself off from the outside world
+ The Rod = communication problems
+ The Mountain = overcoming problems

Card 7 • The Flowers

+ The Heart = intense and genuine love
+ The Park + The Dog = beautiful and good friendships
+ The Bear + The Rod = emotional manipulation
+ The Lion + The Rider = negative news
+ The Lion + The Rider + Amor = a negative love message
+ The Letter + The Book = gathering insights
+ The Snake + The Fox = hypocritical people around you

Card 8 • The Scythe

+ The Heart = a relationship break-up
+ The Dog = the end of a friendship
+ The Flower + The Mice = loss of values and norms
+ The Ship + The Mice + The Coffin = loss or termination of a business
+ The Star = the success is short-lived
+ The Tower + The Cat = watch out for blockages and pride

Card 9 • The Birds

+ The Dog = enemies around you
+ The Moon = unreliable people at work
+ The Book + Amor = secrets in the relationship
+ The Pig = ambitions are not realized
+ The Rider = negative messages
+ The House = unfortunate home
+ The Letter = unexpected setbacks
+ The Fish = financial problems are on the way

Card 10 • The Pig

+ The Moon = ambitions that become reality
+ The Children = beautiful friendships
+ The Fish = financial success
+ The Stork + The House = successful move
+ The Book + The Moon = a positive revelation at work
+ The Ring + The Heart = a stable and happy relationship
+ The Clouds + The Book + The Key + The Ring = relationship solutions
+ The Anchor = lasting and stable happiness

Card 11 • The Fox

+ The Heart = an unreliable lover
+ The Ring = an unreliable partner
+ Hand in Hand = distrust and insecurity
+ The Tower + The Clouds = a separation is made
  more difficult
+ The Mountain = overcoming problems
+ The Scythe + The Clover = being confused with your
  own emotions
+ The Ship = do not trust a potential business partner
+ The Roses + The Tree = being uncertain about
  your appearance

Card 12 • The Children

+ The Mountain = problems with your own child
+ The Clouds = a child has emotional complications
+ The Park = nice social contacts
+ The Heart + The Ring = a loving relationship
+ The Rod = discussion and struggle with your own child or
  a younger person
+ The Broken Glass = the contact with a child is ended
+ The Bride = a child leads a turbulent life

Card 13 • The Snake

+ The Bride = watch out for a rival
+ The Fox + The Bride = watch out for a seductress
+ The Heart + The Bride = watch out for a single lady who
  sabotages your relationship
+ The Lion + The Shepherd = pent up feelings
+ The Shepherd + The Fox = beware of lies

+ The Moon + The Fish = watch out for lack of appreciation at work
+ The Money Safe + The Fish = pay attention when you lend money
+ The Letter + The Fox = check out the fine print in an agreement

Card 14 • The Rider

+ The Heart = a love message
+ The Moon + The Fish = message about promotion at work (or salary increase)
+ The Rod = messages that lead to discussions
+ The Railroad + The Dog = a trip with a friend (can also be a city trip)
+ The Money Safe + The Star = positive messages in business ventures
+ The Eye + The Dog = great friends who show genuine interest in you
+ The Lion + The Bear = watch out for displays of power

Card 15 • The Letter

+ The Heart + The Ring = an unexpected declaration of love
+ The Star = happiness that comes to you unexpectedly
+ The Park + The Heart = pleasant moments with a beloved person
+ The Cat + The Fox = watch out for blackmail
+ The Rapiers + The Tower = watch out for verbal aggression
+ The Lightning + The Flames = negativity is neutralized
+ The Coffin + The Rider = sudden, unfavorable circumstances
+ The Clouds + The Flowers = a confusing message

Card 16 • The Ship

+ The Railroad = vacation
+ The Fish + The House = being self-employed
+ The Rider + The Letter = positive financial news in the mail
+ The Stork + The House = a move or a change in the
  current home
+ The Ship + The Children + The Rider = a pregnancy
+ The Lightning + The Clouds = a negative collaboration
+ The Railroad + The Heart = a journey with a loved one

Card 17 • The Fish

+ The Money Safe = financial profit
+ The Money Safe + The Mice = financial loss
+ The Ship = a successful business
+ The Money Safe + The Rod + The Tower = a fine,
  the state
+ The Railroad + The Ship = work abroad
+ The Book + The Flowers = new ideas regarding work
+ The Lily + The House = virtue in the family circle
+ The Lily + The Lightning + The Broken Glass = family
  quarrels and enmity

Card 18 • The Lady

+ The Heart = a new lover for the female querent
+ The Tower = the lady closes herself off
+ The Snake + The Fox = the lady is not reliable
+ The Bride = the lady is bitter
+ The Flames + Hand in Hand = a loving and sincere lady
+ The Dog + The Anchor + The Ring = a lasting relationship
+ The Rod + The Bear = a verbally overbearing woman

Card 19 • The Gentleman

+ The Heart = a new lover for the male querent
+ The Ship + The Money Safe = this man is wealthy
+ The Bear + The Tower = the man is dominant and overbearing
+ The Fox + The Snake + The Heart = the man is cheating
+ The Bear + Amor + The Sun = the man is genuinely in love
+ The Lightning + The Broken Glass = this man is not good for you
+ The Eye + The Bear + The Tower = this man spies on you, likes to check everything

Card 20 • The Lily

+ The Clouds = family issues that cause sorrow
+ The Coffin + The House = distancing yourself from the family
+ The Birds + The Fox = slander, gossip
+ The Book + The Snake = secrets arising
+ The Stork + The House = taking a new path in the existing family

Card 21 • The Stork

+ The Moon = change of work
+ The House + The Scythe = a move will not take place
+ The Heart + The Children + The Rider = a wish to have a child is fulfilled
+ The Ship + The House = a move abroad
+ The Book + The Fox = things that are kept under the radar
+ The Lion + The Rod + The Ring = fights and struggles with your beloved

+ The Star + The Flowers = a wish coming true

Card 22 • The Book

+ person card = things come to light that are to your advantage
+ The Moon = revelations at work
+ The Dog + The Snake = you will find out who your bad
  friends are
+ The Broken Glass + The Lightning = an irreversible sadness
+ The Birds + The Snake = gossip
+ The Wine = enjoying the little things
+ The Roses + The Tower = external shortcomings
+ The Tree + The Fox + The Snake = obsessive jealousy

Card 23 • The Ring

+ The Scythe = the end of the marriage
+ Amor + The Scythe = the end of the relationship
+ The Heart + The Rod = conflicting feelings of love (not
  knowing what you want)
+ The Flowers = a stable relationship
+ The Ship + The Railroad = a holiday with the partner
+ The Bear = a controlling relationship
+ The Eye + The Tower = a controlling partner
+ The Fox + The Snake + The Lightning = toxic and
  catastrophic relationship problems
+ The Flames + The Heart = a passionate relationship

Card 24 • Hand in Hand

+ The Ship = a reliable work relationship
+ The Ship + The Moon = positive compromises
+ The Clouds + The Mice = don't be too trusting

+ The Snake + The Lightning = unexpected dishonesty

+ The Order = you are appreciated for what you do, gratitude

+ The Lion + The Clouds = being scolded

Card 25 • The Clouds

+ The Ring = distance between two lovers

+ The Heart + Amor = feelings are pent up

+ The Fish + The Rod = financial headaches

+ The Children + The Rod = problems with a child

+ The Star + The Broken Glass = failure

+ The Lightning + The Ship = bankruptcy

+ The Rapiers = be on your guard, threats

Card 26 • The Park

+ The Dog = sincere and beautiful friendships

+ The Lily + The Flowers = popularity

+ The Lightning + The Tower = exaggerating with social contacts

+ The Heart + The Ring = a new lover

+ The Moon + The Snake + The Fox = keeping work and private life separate

+ The Flames + The Star = appreciation for who you are

+ The Rapiers = be on your guard

Card 27 • The Dog

+ The Snake = false friends

+ The Heart + The Fox = a false lover

+ The Star + The Park = beautiful friendships

+ The Mice = loss of friendships

+ The Scythe = ending friendship

+ The Broken Glass = friends that we cannot count on, no interaction
+ The Order + The Moon = appreciation at work, you are rewarded for what you do

Card 28 • The Anchor

+ The Ring = a lasting relationship
+ The House = a stable home
+ The Snake + The Fox = permanent enemies around you
+ The Coffin + The Dog = distancing yourself from friends
+ The Park + The Key = the solution is to be more outgoing
+ The Lion = bad news
+ The Shepherd = genuine affection
+ The Bear + person card = the partner is a permanently dominant person

Card 29 • The Mice

+ The Moon = loss of work
+ The Fish = loss of money or material things
+ The Money Safe = pay attention to how you spend your money, monetary loss
+ The Heart = loss of a loved one
+ The Ring = distance between two people
+ The Dog = trust is being damaged
+ The Pig = an unfortunate situation
+ The Birds = heavy words and arguments

Card 30 • The Rod

+ The Roads = a conflict about a choice
+ The Heart = arguments with a loved one

+ The Dog = arguments with friends
+ The Moon = disagreements at work
+ The Mountain = enemies and problems
+ Amor = our current relationship is under pressure

Card 31 • The Roads

+ The Moon = a work-related choice
+ The Ring = a relationship-related choice
+ The Rod = not being able to make a choice
+ The Tower = blockage when making a choice
+ The Flames = making the right choice
+ The Stork + The House = a choice with regards to a move

Card 32 • The Mountain

+ The Money Safe = money problems
+ The Moon = problems at work
+ The Children = a problem with a child
+ The Flowers = struggling with your own feelings
+ The Clouds + The Lightning + The Heart = catastrophic consequences in the relationship
+ The Scythe + The Ring = not knowing whether to end the relationship
+ The Tree + The Roses = being obsessively concerned with appearances
+ The House = not being happy with the current housing situation

Card 33 • The Clover

+ The Clouds = don't get rushed
+ The Ring + The Dog = a genuine relationship

+ The Sun = success

+ The Key + The Book = solutions are coming soon

+ The Children = don't be too naive

+ The Birds + The Snake = watch out for gossip

Card 34 • The Star

+ The Moon = success at work

+ The Fish = financial prosperity

+ The House + The Stork = a positive move

+ Amor = a successful relationship

+ The Ship = success in all undertakings

+ The Railroad = a correct choice

Card 35 • The Tower

+ The Clover = blocked feelings

+ person card = our partner feels blocked

+ The Moon = a blockage at work

+ The Rapiers = threats

+ The Lightning + The Money Safe = loss of money

+ The Broken Glass + The Ship = the end of a business

+ The Shepherd = false affection

+ The Cat = someone who likes to be in the spotlight

Card 36 • The Cat

+ The Moon = an arrogant person at work

+ The Rapiers = unexpected insults

+ The Ring + Amor = a stubborn partner

+ The Rod + The Clover = to be tangled up

+ The Broken Glass = stubbornness leads to a drastic end

+ The Lightning = pride causes unpleasant surprises

+ The Bride = turbulent love troubles
+ The Dog = watch out for friends who are not sincere
+ The Rapiers + Amor = insulting each other, discussions
  with your loved one

Card 37 • The Rapiers

+ The Star = happiness is short-lived
+ The Moon = emotional complications
+ The Fish + The Money Safe = watch out for financial trouble
+ Amor = the relationship is threatened by insults
+ The Ring + The Fox = the relationship is not based on trust
+ The Wine = plans are canceled
+ The Roses = issues with self-worth

Card 38 • The Flames

+ The Dog + The Heart = lasting love
+ The Dog + The Ring = a stable and good relationship
+ The Dog + Amor = the partners love each other very much
+ The Park + The Heart = a new lover is entering your life
+ The Fish + The Ship = a business becomes successful
+ The Anchor = lasting and stable happiness
+ The Mice = the loss can be prevented
+ The Snake + The Book = timely revelations that prevent a
  catastrophic end

Card 39 • The Heart

+ The Ring = a good and stable relationship
+ Amor = beautiful moments with your partner
+ The Park + The Dog = going out with friends
+ The Park = the arrival of a new lover

+ The Ship + The Fish + The Key = financial and work-related solutions (positive)
+ The Children + The Ring = a youthful partner
+ The Heart + The Lily + The House = positivity in and around the home

Card 40 • The Wine

+ The Park = joyful moments with friends
+ The Heart = joyful moments with your loved one
+ The Lightning = the joyful moments have a catastrophic end
+ The Rod + The Dog = discussions with friends and acquaintances
+ The Fish = enrichment
+ The Roses + The Tree = being in good company
+ The House = feeling good at home

Card 41 • The Roses

+ The Park = wanting to be admired for your looks
+ The Heart = a beautiful bond of love
+ The Tower + The Rod = blocked self-esteem
+ The Rapiers + The Cat = watch out for insults from people around you
+ The Star + The Tree = wanting to look good
+ The Fish + The Ship = appreciation with regards to business activities

Card 42 • Amor

+ The Lightning = unpleasant love surprises
+ The Ring = sudden events with regards to relationships

+ The Broken Glass = an irreversible end of a relationship
+ The Scythe = a break-up of a relationship
+ The Order = recognition in the relationship, gratitude
+ The Flames = a passionate love commitment
+ The Rod = disagreements with your loved one
+ The Tower + partner card = the partner closes off, builds
  a wall around them

Card 43 • The Lightning

+ The Fish = a financial bummer
+ The Star = shattered success
+ The Ship = the company is confronted with sudden problems
+ The Children = problems with a child
+ Amor = unpleasant surprises in love
+ The Broken Glass = the damage cannot be repaired
+ The Letter = bad news
+ The Rider = you receive a negative message
+ The Bride = an unstable lady
+ The Dog = an irreparable friendship

Card 44 • The Broken Glass

+ The Heart = a love relationship is falling apart
+ The Fish = financial loss
+ The Bride = happiness won't be achieved
+ The Ship = the end of a business
+ The Roads = no decisions are made
+ The Key = no solutions are found
+ The Roses = external defects
+ The Stork = the move is postponed
+ The Mountain = difficulties are piling up

Card 45 • The Order

+ The Heart = recognition of love
+ The Letter = a love letter
+ The Rider = a love message
+ The Ship + The Fish = the business makes profit
+ The Star = lasting success
+ The Bride = a loving and grateful lady
+ The Stork + The House = a move and being self-employed

Card 46 • The Railroad

+ The Ship = a holiday or trip
+ The Heart + The Ship = a holiday with a loved one
+ The Broken Glass = not paying attention on the road, driving under the influence
+ The Fish + The Ship = foreign collaboration
+ The Letter = a message from abroad
+ The Money Safe = a transaction from abroad
+ The Money Safe + The Rod = make sure that you don't spend money on someone abroad
+ The Money Safe + The Scythe = you will not get the money back

Card 47 • The Bride

+ The Moon = a lonely lady
+ The Snake = an unreliable lady or rival
+ The Fox + The Heart = a seductress
+ The Money Safe + The Fish + The Order = a wealthy lady, a hard worker
+ The Ship + The Dog = a vacation with a female friend
+ The Eye + The Flowers = someone is interested in you
+ The Book + The Key = the goals will be achieved

Card 48 • The Money Safe

(pay attention to the placement of the open and closed side of the safe)

+ The Rod = financial struggle
+ The Scythe = financial loss
+ The Tower = blockage with regards to finances
+ The Coffin + The Mice = loss of money, payment of fines
+ The Lightning = unpleasant, financial surprises
+ The Flowers + The Eye + The Order = financial prosperity

Card 49 • The Eye

+ The Park = a party with friends
+ partner card + The Book = secrets in the relationship are revealed
+ The Snake = avoid unreliable people before it's too late
+ The Fox = seeing through false people
+ The Moon = introspection
+ The Tree = stable health
+ The Coffin = an unexpected revelation

Card 50 • The Bear

+ partner card = an overbearing partner
+ The Snake = lies and deceit
+ The Fox = don't get involved with people who are dishonest
+ The Lion = shocking events
+ The Bride = a dominant lady
+ Amor = a relationship based on power
+ The House + The Lily = an unhealthy situation at home

Card 51 • The Lion

\+ The Heart = bad news from a loved one
\+ The Letter = bad news in the mail
\+ The Rod = a serious discussion
\+ The Scythe + The Sun = happiness is short-lived
\+ The Shepherd = the affection is not what it should be
\+ The Fish = financial worry

Card 52 • The Shepherd

\+ Amor = an intense crush
\+ The Stork + Amor = a move with the partner
\+ The Heart = to have compassion for someone else
\+ The Rider + The Park = beautiful and genuine social contacts
\+ The Moon = frivolity
\+ The Children = naivety

8
Important guidelines for consulting the Gypsy Cards

Unfortunately, I often notice that people are more inclined to come up with inventive stories that are not always 100% consistent with the truth. Try to be as honest as possible, even if you see things that are not pleasant. Everyone benefits from substantiated and honest advice, especially in challenging or unfavorable situations. So, don't avoid them, but do offer solutions. Always give readings as you would like to receive readings yourself!

And further...

- Never talk about death.
- Never talk about complex health issues.
- Never make choices instead of the querent.
- Never say anything to spare the other person.
- Stay loyal and kind.
- Always indicate that you are doing your best to answer as honestly as possible.
- We are not God and do not see what will happen in five years.
- You give advice and an indication. The other person decides what to do with it.
- Don't make up stories.
- Practice often before you start reading for other people.
- Take your time.
- Don't read cards when you are not feeling well.
- Give yourself the time and space to grow.

We have arrived at the end of *Reading Fortune Telling Cards.*
The Romani people inspired me in a very fascinating way
when I was a little boy. I personally think their way of predicting is amazing. They like to distinguish themselves from
others and that is what you should do as a person and as a
card reader.

Some questions and situations are complex, and it is therefore up to us, card readers, to make a good and correct
assessment of how we will be conveying the story. Some
people like a confrontational approach, while others prefer a
gentler approach. However, remain honest in your final conclusion and don't tell people merely what they want to hear.

A card reading shows us a path that we can take, highlights
possible stumbling blocks and gives us the information that
we need at that moment. It is a special and fascinating but at
the same time quite heavy matter, because we penetrate the
world of the other person. Card reading can be compared to
a puzzle that you, as the reader, are putting together for the
querent. You help someone to gain insights that they can't
find elsewhere.

With this book I have tried to teach you the Romani approach
to divination and to enable you to explore the depths of your
subconscious. By doing this, you will enter an extremely fascinating world that includes more than just cards.

I wish you a lot of success in studying the Gypsy cards. And
... I hope that you will experience the same fascination and
satisfaction I have enjoyed.

Good luck!
Fabio Vinago

Notes

Notes

For our complete line of tarot decks,
books, meditation cards, oracle sets,
and other inspirational products
please visit our website:

www.usgamesinc.com

Follow us on:

U.S. GAMES SYSTEMS, INC.
179 Ludlow Street
Stamford, CT 06902 USA
Phone: 203-353-8400
Order Desk: 800-544-2637
FAX: 203-353-8431